How to Open a Sober Living Home

Help Others Get Back on Track to Living a Fulfilling Life

Caiden Delaney

Please consult a licensed professional before attempting any techniques outlined in this book.

By reading this document, the reader agrees that under no circumstances is the author responsible for any losses, direct or indirect, that are incurred as a result of the use of information contained within this document, including, but not limited to, errors, omissions, or inaccuracies.

Table of Contents

Introduction

Addiction. Maybe it's something you've dealt with in the past or maybe you've been fortunate enough to have not struggled with it. Even if you haven't, my guess is that you know of someone who is or has struggled with an addiction at some point in their life. It's no surprise for me to say that most people aren't successful in their rehab process. It's for the simple reason that recovery is a much longer process than 30 days for example. You can't go from a controlled environment to being completely on your own and not expect bad habits or temptation to start to creep back in. Luckily this is where something like a sober living or transitional house can come into play. These places can help people start to get back on their feet without the pressure of being completely thrust back into the world on their own. Not only is this very helpful to people, but you can make some good income off of it as well. By the end of this book, you'll have the knowledge you need to open and successfully run your own sober living home. There are a lot of things that I need to cover, so why waste another second?

Chapter 1: This is About More Than the Money

The first thing I want you to think about is why. Why do you want to open up a sober living, transitional, halfway house, or whatever else you want to call it? Do you have a heart for helping people in need? Have you been a former addict yourself? Do you think it's a great opportunity to make money? I'm not here to say there's anything wrong with being purely motivated by the money! However, you do have to keep in mind that it's going to take a lot of patience to be able to be successful in this business. Having that compassion for others will help you get through the tough challenges that you will inevitably face when dealing with people who are in recovery. There will be people who relapse. There will be people who try to sneak things into the house that they shouldn't. Honestly, if you're purely motivated by the money, you could look into real estate to rent out to a family. If you are able to stay patient, then I know that you will be rewarded greatly for it. Not just with compensation, but with seeing people overcome their addictions and be able to get back on a path to normalcy. Take myself as an example. I started drinking back when I was in high school. I wanted a way to socialize and to fit in with my peers. I also come from a small town where there isn't a whole lot else to do. So naturally, binge drinking kind of became my norm. That trend would continue with me into college. The thing is you would think that after I had dropped out of college, I would start to slow down and focus more on a career and a family. At that point though, the habit was so ingrained in me, that I found myself drinking whenever I had the time. Before and after work on the weekdays and all throughout the day on the weekends. It wasn't uncommon for me to be able to clear through a 30-pack of beer in one day or even more if I was around the right people. I always thought that I was functioning like a normal person, but you never know how your life can suddenly change in an instant. At the time I was working as a forklift operator, and I wasn't paying attention and crashed the forklift into some racking while I had a full load. So I of course had to get tested for drugs and alcohol to ensure that the accident was unrelated to me operating the machinery while under the influence. As you can guess, that didn't go so well and I found myself unemployed. At the time, my girlfriend and I's financial situation wasn't the worst but it wasn't the best either. I could get by for a couple of weeks if I had to. Unemployment wasn't going to be an option due to the incident, but I felt confident that I could get a job soon enough. The problem was that I had no motivation to apply for jobs. All I could seem to focus on was picking up the next beer. Soon enough, weeks turned into months and I was still spending my days sitting on the couch drinking. I knew what I should have been doing, but I just couldn't get myself to do it. Now the heat was on in terms of our financial situation. We began to start to fight about our financial situation more than I care to admit. Nothing ever turned physically violent, which I'm proud to say. However, things had boiled up to a point where my girlfriend could no longer handle the constant tension. Why should she be with someone who can't take care of her let alone take care of himself? She had enough on her plate as it was, and I was only magnifying the stress levels. She loved me and I knew that she did, but she had to do what was best for both of us and that was moving on. Losing my job was one thing, but losing my girl...that's a whole different level of hurt. When I lost my job, I at least had her to support me emotionally and financially through the tough times. Now I had nobody, except for one thing...the alcohol. So naturally, that's what I turned to even more than I had before. I was holding a beer more often than I wasn't. To say I was depressed was an understatement. Paying my rent wasn't a thing, so I moved back in with my parents. I'm grateful to have had the opportunity to be able to do that or else I would have been homeless. Naturally though, my bad habit started to wear on my parents. I wanted to get better, I really did, so through the help of my parents, I was able to participate in some out-patient treatment programs. The programs were great, don't get me wrong, the problem was that I was back in my home town, which meant I was right back around the same people where my habit began. The hold that alcohol had on me was stronger than ever before. I knew the only way I was going to be successful was to leave the current environment I was in. So my parents and I decided to send me to an in patient program that was 4 hours away from where they lived. This way I would be able to focus solely on my recovery and not be around the crowd that would temp me to go back into my old ways. It was when I was in the in-patient program that I learned about a sober living home that was in the same city. I really thought this would be a good transition for me. Once I complete the in patient program, if I moved back in with my parents, I'd be in the same environment again. If I was out on my own completely, then I would have struggled financially, mentally, and emotionally having no support system around me. So I ended up moving into the sober home and living their for 18 months to really help me get back on my feet. I'm proud to say that I haven't looked back and that was a little over 12 years ago as I'm writing this book. If it wasn't for my parents and everything they did to support me, then I wouldn't have been able to overcome this battle. Their love and patience for me won the day, and now I get to be that beam of shining light for others. You see, this is why you have to be patient with the people you're working with. They're going to need time to heal and you need to be that person who can be patient with them along the way instead of walking away. My story is what inspired me to want to start my own sober living home. I have the experience to know what it's like to suffer from the grips that addiction can take on someone. I know how hard it can become to overcome the odds, especially without a solid support system in place. This is why I'm so grateful to have the opportunity that I do to be able to make a difference in the world that I feel is truly impactful. The money is secondary to me. Nothing gives me energy quite like hearing someone tell me that their live is forever changed thanks to me. If you've had a moment like that before, then you know just how good of a feeling it is. It's why I spring out of bed every morning ready to go. So needless to say, starting this business wasn't about the money for me in the beginning. As things have grown, I'm not going to lie it is nice to see the income follow along with the impact. Money does make a difference and don't let anyone tell you otherwise. When it comes to addiction, it really is a double edge sword. It can get you into trouble, but it can also help with recovery. No matter what your motivation is for wanting to open a halfway house, I want to give you the necessary information you need to set yourself up for success. Before I get into the finer details, I want to share with you some of the other reasons why I think this business makes sense purely from a business standpoint.

You Can Make More Money From Each Asset

Your goal could be to own one sober living home and leave it at that, or you could open up multiple sober living homes and scale the business. Either way, the cool thing is that you can make more money per house than you would if you were to rent it out to a normal family. Real estate prices will vary greatly depending on where you live, but no matter where you live, you can squeeze a lot of juice from your real estate assets by turning them into sober living homes. Let's say a 3 bedroom 2 bathroom home in your area would rent for $2,000 per month, assuming one family would be renting it. You could rent that same house out and make $3,000 per month by having 6 people live there as part of your sober living home. Even if this was a situation where roommates would be living in a home, people typically don't share rooms. Even in cases where they would such as college students, the rent is still lower. You're not charging based on the number of rooms in the home. Your pricing is based on the number of beds in the house. You could do the same number of beds per room, but possibly fit an extra one in the master bedroom depending on the house. Therefore you can make the most out of the square footage that's in the home way more than a normal rental can.

Drug and Alcohol Addiction Isn't Going Anywhere

This point is unfortunate, but it is true. Drug and alcohol addiction isn't going anywhere. I wish this wasn't the case and that it would disappear for good, but realistically I know that's never going to be the case. This means that there will always be a need for transitional housing. People become addicted to substances for various reasons: boredom, peer pressure, trying to fit in to seem cool, hanging around the wrong crowd, coping with loss or hardship, etc. It's for these reasons among many others that will keep the demand in tact. You'll always have someone in your area that is in need of help, so as long as they're able to find you or you're able to find them, you'll keep the beds in your home full. If this is something you find yourself struggling with, then it likely has more to do with your marketing ability then a lack of demand.

Not as Active as Other Businesses

One great thing about being in the real estate field is that real estate is a form of semi-passive income. In fact, you could make this business virtually passive if you put the right team members in place. Until you reach that point though, there is work to be done even after you have the house. You're going to have to do some prep work to get things ready, you're going to have to market your home to fill up the beds, there's going to be maintenance repairs that need to be done on the home, and manage your tenets. However, if you put the right systems and processes in place, a lot of these things will take care of themselves, or at the very least will take up less of your time. When someone is living at your property, they're paying you just to stay there. You still own the asset and you don't have to put in much work to earn the rent money.

Chapter 2: Getting Your Name Out There

The first thing I want to talk about before anything else is marketing your sober living home. That may sound like I'm putting the cart before the horse. Shouldn't you establish the business first or actually have a home for people to live in? Yes, it seems backwards, but it's not. Marketing your company is free. Buying the home, furnishing it, establishing the business, etc., those things are not free. You don't want to get everything set up just to hear crickets. You want to put yourself out there to start letting people know you exist. Some people might be ready right when you talk to them, and they'll have to wait. Others though won't be ready, but they will be when you open, which is exactly what you want. Consider the worst case scenario, which is you talk to someone and they're ready to move in, but you're not. Well if you didn't speak to them and instead focused solely on getting the house ready, then they never would've talked to you, they still wouldn't know who you are, and thus they wouldn't be moving in anyways. You have to get to people before they are ready because in some cases people need time to figure out what their next move is going to be. Do you let your apartment lease end and then try to find a new place to live? No, you plan out months in advance if you're resigning or leaving. If you leave, you give yourself time to search. Now imagine if you were 2 months away from moving out and you were exposed to another complex's marketing materials. I'm willing to bet you'd check them out because they'd be hitting you at the right time. You never know who you'll be talking to where it could be perfect timing for things to line up for when you open. The only way you'll know is by putting yourself out into the world before you feel fully ready. I know you're not ready and that's okay. Don't let your mind trick you into stalling, you need to market your home from day one!

Fish in the Right Spot

If you wanted to catch a saltwater fish, would it be a wise idea to go fishing in a pond for this kind of fish you want? Obviously, it wouldn't be because you'd need to fish in the ocean to catch a saltwater fish. Fishing from a freshwater source will do you no good. That seems silly, but people make this mistake in marketing all of the time. They are marketing in places where their customers are not at. Their customers will never get the message and the business will stay stuck. It's no different than trying to catch a saltwater fish in a freshwater pond. I bring this up because when it comes to a sober living home, there are a lot of ways you can find yourself fishing in the wrong spot. It may seem like you're in the right spot, but you're way off and your home will stay empty because of it. The following are some of the ways you can market your business that may sound good in theory, but will waste time and money in the beginning.

Running Ads

Advertising your business works, I'm not trying to deny that. However, doing this at the start, especially for this type of business is not the most effective way to go about things. Advertising on a platform, be it the radio, TV, or social media, will cost you money. With radio and TV ads, it can be harder to hit your target demographic unless you know the type of music or shows they like to watch. Let's face it though, people suffering from addiction don't just listen to one type of music or a certain channel. It could be anyone that you're trying to appeal to. This makes it hard to narrow down as you're advertising to a more general audience. You also have to think about what you're going to say in your ad. It has to be compelling enough to make someone want to take action, which can be hard to do if you have no experience running ads. Most advertisers have to spend quite a bit of money testing things to come across something that works. When it does work, it pays off big time, that's the way it goes. It's very possible that you don't have a big budget for ads and even if you do, there are better ways to spend your time and money. With social media ads, you can make things more targeted, but again, how do you know if you're putting yourself directly in front of your ideal customers? The one exception I would have to this would be something such as online search ads. You can run an ad to rank at the top of the first page for a keyword that someone types in. For example, someone might type in "out-patient treatment program near me." Your ad will put your website at or near the top for that phrase when it's searched. This is highly targeted because people searching for this are in need of treatment. You can run multiple ads to help cover a wide variety of keywords. With this being said, it's still going to cost money and take time to tweak things for optimization. There are free and effective ways to market your sober living home that should be explored first before you start running online search ads.

Creating Social Media Business Pages

Starting up social media pages feels like a good thing to do. It gives you a warm and fuzzy feeling on the inside. Much like running ads though, it can be hard to get your message in front of the right people. Additionally, you have to work quite hard just to build up enough of a following to get eyeballs on your content. Your home is also location bound. So you'd want your followers to be in locations where your homes are. Gaining followers from people that live too far away are useless the majority of the time. This is a common mistake younger business owners make. They focus their attention on the wrong things, such as trying to build a following to look cool to their peers. We're building a business here, not a big following online! Specifically in this case, you have to consider that sober homes aren't always welcomed with open arms in the community. It's sometimes better to fly under the radar and not let certain people know you exist. One thing I will say is that you could fill up beds with social media, but you'd be relying on someone in need or a family member/close friend of someone in need to see your post. Yes, it's possible, but you're basically casting a wide net and hoping to catch a particular fish. You can instead fish in a small pond that only contains the type of fish that you're looking for.

How Should You Get Your Beds Full?

Now that you know of a few things you shouldn't be focusing your energy on, where should you pay attention to? Your attention needs to be put into getting yourself directly in front of the people you want to serve. Go to the places where your customers are and talk to them. This means going to local treatment centers, sobriety meetings, hospitals, social workers, jails and prisons, etc. The places you want to visit first would be things such as sobriety meetings and treatment centers. People at these places have shown that they care about making a change in their life. This means you're not going to have to convince these people that they need to change. They know this and have already taken action towards changing for the better. Other places can be more hit or miss, but your target customer will be there so it's worth getting your name out there. For instance, someone might be in jail because of their addiction. They still may not care to change. Or it could be that because they ended up doing time, they are now motivated to make changes in their life. You won't know until you try. So how do you put yourself in front of these people? Well, it's not going to be practical to go and speak to every individual that's at one of these places. Instead, you're going to be much better off building connections with the people operating these facilities. Once you have a connection with the right people, they'll start to refer people to you right and left. The best place to start would be any place that you have an affiliation with. Maybe you've been a part of a sobriety group before or have been in a treatment center before. Maybe you know someone who has gone through a treatment center before. You want to use this connection to your advantage because you already have your foot in the door. In this case, you already know who you need to talk to in order to let them know about your home. Simply give that contact a call or stop by and see them in person. Explain to them how the treatment center had such a big impact on your journey. Talk about how being sober has had such a big impact on your life, which is why you decided to open up your own sober living home. Then tell them that you have some open spots you're looking to fill, offer to leave them with your business card, and that you'd be grateful for anyone they send your way. Even if you don't know of anyone at a center or other such place, the process is virtually the same. You want to go to these various places and explain to them your story and how you came to open your halfway house. This is an important part of the process because it will allow the other person to see the passion within your heart. Leave them with your information and tell them you'd be thankful for anyone they could send your way. Most of the time, you'll end up speaking to someone working the front desk and that's okay. If you can find the person in charge of running the meetings or managing the facility, that would be better, but you're not always going to be able to. Don't let that hold you back from stopping by and talking to as many places as you can. This is going to be your ticket to filling up your home without having to spend any money. If you're not filling up spots the way you'd like to, then ask yourself how many places you've talked to in the past week. Chances are good that it hasn't been enough. I get that it may seem a little scary, but believe it or not people aren't going to be rude to you in most cases. They'll be able to see that you're authentic and trying to help others in need. You don't need to memorize a script or anything like that. It's about stopping at every place you can more than anything else. There is no better way to get your home out there when you're first starting, so don't try to stall and find another way. The payout will be worth any apprehension that you feel. There are people that are counting on you to do this because they won't recover unless you get your name out there. Stop and think about that. People's addictions will continue on if you don't market yourself to the best of your ability. So take full responsibility for this and start hustling!

Keep in Contact

Once you do have people live in your home, they're not going to stay with you forever, even if you would allow them to. Eventually, people will move out. As sad as it is for me to say, some of the people who move out will slip back into their old ways. It likely won't happen immediately, but over the months and years it will occur to some of the people you come across. This essentially is your business' version of having a repeat customer. Sometimes they will reach back out to you or one of their loved ones will. You don't want to wait around for them to give you a call that may never come. This is why you need to reach out and see how they're doing. This is just the right thing to do because you should care to see how they're doing. Hopefully, they're still on the right path. If they are, great! They'll appreciate the call, and you'll stay at the back of their mind in case relapse does occur. You could call and they're relieved that you did because they relapsed and they need help. This is business you wouldn't have generated if you didn't call. You don't want to bother someone every week asking how they're doing. There's also no specific way to go about it. Gauge it based on the person. You could reach out to someone every 3-6 months to check in on them and ensure they're staying on the sober path. You never know what will come from it, so reach out to every person that has stayed with you previously!

What Type of Home Do You Want to Have?

In order to have a successful sober living home, you need to determine what type of home you want to have. What I mean by this is do you want to have a home where the roommates form a close bond and work together on their journeys? Or do you want something where everyone is more so maintaining their own space and doing their own thing? I'm not saying that either approach is wrong, but you need to define the type of home you'll be because mixing these two groups can create tension. Imagine if you have a group of tight-knit roommates in a home and then someone moves in who wants to go about things in their own way. How well do you think that person is going to get along with everyone else? The person will mess with the vibe that the rest of the housemates have and it can create tension in the home. If you know from the beginning what type of home you want to have, then you can avoid this issue. You'll be able to see what people's goals are and what they're looking to achieve from living in your home. You can focus on accepting people that are in alignment with how you want your home to function.

Sober Living Home Intake Form

This leads me to the next point, which is your client intake form. This is essentially someone submitting an application to see if they'd be a good fit for your sober living home. Think of it like applying to live in an apartment. An apartment complex doesn't just accept anyone who applies. They're careful about who they let in because they don't want to deal with a bad tenant who won't pay their rent. You need to follow this premise as well. It can be tempting to accept anyone who applies, but you have to think about the current group's best interest before you accept just anyone. Your intake form will be used to help guide your decision-making process on who you will accept and who you will deny. It can be tempting to take on anyone who's willing in the beginning, but it's better to do your own due diligence and make the proper discernment. This person is going to be living in your home with other people and that's a big responsibility. So what are some questions you should ask on your form to get a good gauge for the type of person applying to live in your home? The following are some recommendations:

What Are You Hoping to Achieve by Staying Here?

With this question, you're not looking for one specific answer. You're more so looking for something that shows initiative for the person to improve themselves. So someone might say they want to work on themselves, focus on their recovery, stay clean, etc. These are all perfectly acceptable answers. If someone were to answer and stay they're just looking for a place to live so they're not homeless, that's a bit of a red flag. They may not care to stay sober and could be a bad influence to the other people living in the home.

Do You Prefer to Recover By Yourself or in a Group Setting?

This ties in with what I was just talking about. You want to get an understanding for how the person wants to approach their recovery journey. By knowing this information, you can help to determine the type of home that you want to form.

How Long Do You Plan on Staying Here For?

You'll accomplish a few things by asking this. One is you need to determine how long you'll allow someone to stay in your home. Do you only allow 6 months, or maybe 12-24 months? Or are people allowed to stay as long as they want if they're paying rent and not causing any trouble? If you only allow people to stay for a year, but someone plans on staying for 18 months, you will know about the misalignment. You can work with the person and explain to them the amount of progress they could make in 12 months. You can see if they'd be interested in only being able to stay for 12 months. This is better than the person figuring out this information later on down the line. Asking this will also give you potential insight into the ambition of the person. Maybe they're eager and they think they'll be good to go after 6 months. It could also be that they have a personal reason that would cause them to move out after 6 months. Lastly, it lets you know about how long the person plans on staying, which allows you to plan around it. You'll know that you could potentially have someone moving out after let's say 6 months, so you'll have a general timeline for when you should start looking to fill the void.

What is Your Support System Currently Like?

This will give you insight into who could potentially help them pay for the rent at your home if the prospective tenant is unable to do so themselves. It also gives you a small peak into the likelihood of them facing relapse. If they don't have a good support system, then they could be more likely to fall back into old habits. If they have loved ones who will continue to support them in their sobriety journey, then chances are much better that they will be able to stay clean. You'll want to keep in contact with anyone who stays at your home, but pay close attention to the people who unfortunately don't have a good support system in the outside world.

How Long Have You Been Clean?

If someone has been clean for a longer period of time, they'll be more likely to continue staying clean because they won't want to ruin their streak. If someone has been clean for only a few days or weeks, then they have less to lose so to speak. Aside from that, different people will be at different phases in their sobriety journey. This may affect your approach in terms of who rooms with who and what type of activities or programs the group participates in. You can also discern if you want people to live in your home who are farther along in their journey or who are more towards the beginning, or if they can be at any stage.

What Drug Addiction Have You Struggled With?

This is just good general information to know, but it can also help you know a little bit more about the people living in your home. This can help you determine who shares a room with who. For instance, you may not want to pair people together who have used the same drug before. On the other hand, you might want to pair them together so they can better bond over a similar struggle.

Have You Been in Jail or Prison Before?

This will be a simple yes or no answer. You want to have some additional questions below in case they answer yes, such as what were you in jail for, how long were you in jail for, and how recently were you released? It may very well be that they were in jail for possession of a controlled substance. This would fit right in with what you'd expect. There are plenty of other reasons why they could be in jail. It could be because of something like assault or theft, for example. You have to draw the line on what you're comfortable with and what you're not. Someone with a prior record of something like assault could create a dangerous situation for the other housemates. The last thing you want is for other people in the home to feel uncomfortable and potentially move out because of it.

What Medications Are You Currently Taking?

This one is interesting because some medications can be abused and this is a sober living home. People need to take their medications though, so it's more about being aware so the proper measurements can be taken. You want to ensure the medications are locked away from the housemates they don't belong to. You also want to keep a close eye on the person the medications are prescribed to as they could still abuse them.

Asking these questions will allow you to quickly gain information about someone, but these aren't the only things you need to think about with your home.

Do People Need to Complete a Program Before You Accept Them?

Some sober living homes will require people to complete an in-patient or out-patient treatment program before they accept them to come and live in the home. Other homes will not have this requirement. So what should you do? It comes down to what you prefer. Not having people complete a program will lower the bar for entry. This will lead to more people applying to live in your home. However, the quality of the tenant will consistently be lower. This isn't to say you can't get good tenants because you certainly will. The people you do get may very well have gone through a treatment program, so you'll have a mix of both if you decide to not make it a requirement. People who have not gone through a treatment program will have a higher chance of being clean for a shorter period of time. They also haven't necessarily demonstrated that they want change and are capable of it. If you do make this a requirement, then you know anyone you get has shown a willingness to change, and that they didn't give up and stuck with it to complete the program. These are great signs and characteristics you want to see in someone who would be living in an asset you bought. So yes, you might get less people to apply, but who cares if you get a bunch of people applying, making it a higher chance you have issues with people in the future. Your job will be a lot easier if you have more trustworthy people living in your homes. This is why I recommend making it a requirement to seek treatment before living in a home.

What Should the Price of Rent Be?

With inflation, the cost of living is increasing. It's worse in some places than others, but no matter what it affects everyone. Your property's value is going to increase. Therefore, your property taxes and insurance will increase, which will increase your monthly mortgage rate. You'll then have to increase the rent to help accommodate for this change. This is the case even if you own a home. So imagine people trying to get back on their feet and get their own place. The cost may simply be too much and they can't afford to live on their own. Lack of housing can make it harder for people to stay on the right path. This is why transitional housing can have a huge advantage. You can come in at a lower price point and it's not because the home is tiny and run down. It's because you'll maximize each room the home has, and you'll be doing so in a way that makes sense. Imagine if you tried to room strangers together with no context to make more money from your home. That would be weird and probably wouldn't turn out too well. So how much should a person be charged per month for the rent? You'll typically see ranges of $450-$600 per month. Real estate prices can vary quite drastically from city to city. However, if you are on the higher end in terms of rent, you can bet that means everywhere else in that area is even pricier. Comparatively, these prices aren't that bad and they look even better when you compare them to what a one-bedroom apartment would cost them. A one-bedroom apartment for $600 in most areas isn't going to be nice if you're even able to find a price that cheap. It's going to be run down and likely needs a lot of maintenance work done. In the area that I live, it's not uncommon for one-bedroom apartments to go for around $1,300 per month. By living in a halfway house, someone could cut that expense down by more than half, and as the owner you're making more money overall, so it's a win for everyone! In order to determine exactly what your rent should be, this will also depend on the loan and what your monthly payments are. You'll want to ensure that you're generating enough cash flow to cover the mortgage every month and have money to set aside for repairs that will inevitably happen. For example, if your mortgage is $2,400 per month for a 4-bedroom home, then you might charge $500 per month. If you house two people to a room, this means at max capacity you'd be making $4,000 per month. This is a good cash flow for a sober house and it also gives you some cushion in case you have some people move out and it takes you a little bit of time to fill the empty spots. You'd also be charging a fair price assuming that your home looks like a place someone would actually want to live! This of course is just an example, but that's my thought process when determining what I want the rent to be. I want a cushion in case some people move out, and I want to be able to set aside some money for repairs. If you're able to do that, then you'll be sitting pretty! The last thing I want to talk about is the amount of people you should put into a home. I briefly touched on this earlier, but now I want to go more in-depth. Since we're running some hypothetical numbers here, it could be tempting to think about having 3 people in a room. Now that same 4-bedroom house could hold 12 people. You could still charge $500 per month and now your making $6,000 per month. You could even lower the rent to $450 and you'd still make $5,400 per month, which is well above the amount for two people per room. There are a few things you have to consider though. The first is the people. Are they going to have as good of an experience and be able to focus on themselves and their recovery if it feels like they're living in a shelter? Of course not! Their recovery is going to be impacted. You want them to have a feeling of independence and ownership, like they have their own space. It's hard to do that when you're cramming more than two people in a room. There's nothing out of the ordinary with two people to a room. Colleges do it, jail cells do it, but three or more people starts to push things. If people feel too cramped in your home, they're going to move out at a faster rate, and you're going to have a lot of different tenants. In the long run, it's not going to be worth the hassle because it's harder to find a new tenant than it is to keep a current one.

Chapter 3: Getting Your First House and Other Considerations to Officially Operate

You now have a good idea for how you can fill up your homes and that comes down to hustling for the most part. The next step is to start handling the business side of things so that you're operating correctly and that you have a home for people to live in. There can be quite a bit that goes into the process, and so I'm going to go over things bit by bit here. Taking in this information in bite-sized chunks is the best approach. If you try to handle everything at once, you're going to get flustered and give up on this idea altogether.

How to Buy Your First Property

The first thing I want to go into is securing your first property. There are other ways you can go about getting a home to use as a sober living house, and I'll cover those later on. For now, I want to hone in on buying a property. This is going to be the best way to go about things in the long run. You'll own the property, which will appreciate in value as time goes on. You'll own the asset, which means you'll have more control over how you want to do things unless the home is part of a homeowner's association, in which case you may have to abide by some of their guidelines. The first step in the process I want you to do is get pre-approved for a loan. This is important to do so that you know what you're looking for and what you can afford. If you start by trying to look at homes first, you'll be wasting your time in most cases. You can stumble across what you believe to be the perfect home only to then realize that you don't qualify to be able to buy it. By doing things in the reverse order, you can help to filter your search so that you're only looking for what is within your range. You can start applying for loans to get pre-approved from various banks, and then you can start to compare the rates to see what the best option is for you. After that, you should reach out to a real estate agent. They'll be able to send you listings, put in offers for you, and help close any deals you and the seller decide to move forward with. The cool thing about a real estate agent is that the seller pays the commission of the sale price. The percentage will vary a little bit, and it's usually divided out amongst the seller's real estate and your real estate agent, but it's covered by the seller. Therefore, it's a no-brainer to use a real estate agent when looking to buy your first home. You can give them the criteria you're looking for in the home, and they can find you listings that you wouldn't have found otherwise. They'll submit offers for you, and once an offer is accepted, that's not the end all be all. Contingencies must be met, and this is an important point to remember. Just because a house is under contract does not mean that the deal will go through. Under contract means that the buyer and seller have agreed to a deal.

Once that happens, the buyer will send in a home inspector to look at the home and see what's wrong with it, and see what repairs need to be done. At this point, this is where the negotiation beings to happen. Let's say a home was listed at $350,000, and you put in an offer for $360,000 that gets accepted. It comes back on the inspection that the roof needs to be replaced and it's going to cost $10,000. It is also discovered that the drain on one of the bathtubs drains slower than it should among other things. At this point, you decide what you care about and what you don't. You might tell your real estate agent that the roof needs to be fixed in order for you to buy at $360,000. The other side might not budge and that's how a deal can fall through. The other side may go ahead and fix it and then the house will eventually close. The other scenario is where they'll deduct the estimated costs of the repair. So in this case, they'd deduct $10,000 from the $360,000 for a new total of $350,000, and then it's on you to get the roof replaced. Everything is up for negotiation. There will be various little things wrong with the home, and you can fight each little thing if you want to, like in the case of a bathtub draining slower than it should. For most of these things though, it's cheap enough to fix on your own so you don't have to worry about a deal falling through. You have to focus on what's a deal breaker for you and what isn't. Some people will list their home at a certain price knowing that some major things are wrong with it and they won't budge on their pricing. You have to simply decide if the deal that's on the table is worth it to you. Depending on what your money situation is like, it could be of benefit for you to buy a cheaper home and repair it yourself to save money. There are a variety of approaches to this, which is great because you don't have to already be rich in order to start changing other people's lives with a sober living home. Once everything is agreed upon and signed, congratulate yourself because the deal is now done! One thing to keep in mind when looking to buy a home is to stay patient, positive, and consistent. You need to consistently look at homes every day so that way you can have an early jump on anything new that pops up. You need to stay positive that your offer will get accepted, and you need to stay patient because it takes time to find a good deal. If you're not looking at homes consistently and putting in offers, then there's no chance of you being able to close a deal. The majority of the offers you put in won't get accepted. If they do, then there's a good chance that you overbid by too much. When you do find a deal that you like, it comes down to your preference, do you want to pay above the listing price to increase the likelihood that your offer gets accepted? Or would you rather be patient by submitting a lower offer and waiting until you have one get accepted? You are running a business here, so if you overpay, that extra money is going to be eating into your profit margins. On the other side though, you may come across a property that checks off every single box for you and you can't afford to let it slip past you, so you submit a strong offer. A lot of your strategy will depend on the area you live in and what the housing market is currently doing. If you're living in an area that's rapidly growing and the selling market is strong, then you will likely have to bid above the listing price in order to have a chance. If you live in an area where the growth is more stagnant and the housing market is calm, then you likely won't have to overbid, and in some cases you may be able to offer below listing if the person is desperate to sell. You also won't have as many homes for sale, so you'll need to analyze every opportunity that comes up more closely.

Renting a Property

If you're not 100% sure about a sober living home and just want to test things out, then you can do that by renting a property instead of buying a home. Buying a home for this purpose will be a good investment, but it might be more of a commitment than you're looking to take on. You may want to test the waters and see what the day-to-day is really like. You want to see if you have what it takes to be able to operate this kind of business. Well, one way you can go about doing that is by renting a place. Most of the time, you'll be looking at a year-long lease. This is plenty of time for you to be able to see if you like what you're doing. Some landlords though will offer a 6-month or even month-to-month lease. With these options, you'll be paying more per month, but you won't have to commit as long. After 3 months, you may realize this business isn't for you. If that ends up being the case, you'd be much happier only having 3 months left or being able to get out of it at the end of the month, rather than having to stay put for another 9 months. Again though, it all depends on the situation and what opportunity presents itself to you. You might find the perfect spot to rent and it happens to be a 12-month lease, so you go ahead and commit due to the location. You also might not be able to find many other options than a 12-month lease. The tricky part when it comes to leasing is what you're using the home for. Landlords are going to be more hesitant to lend their home to someone who wants to use it for the purposes of a transitional home. They don't know the backgrounds of anyone who would be staying in the home, and they'd want to protect their asset. You're essentially trying to overcome preconceived notions. You could try to keep things on the low and not share what your true intentions are with the home. However, the landlord won't be too happy if they find out what's actually going on. I'd rather make things known up front. Sure, it will take you a bit longer to find a home, but once you do, you're at least on the same page with the landlord. If you do find yourself in a desperate situation and no one wants to lease you their home, there are some things you can do to help move things along. The first would be to put down a bigger deposit. This way if something does happen to the house, the landlord will be able to pull from your deposit instead of their own pockets. You could also offer to pay for the 12-month lease upfront if you're able to afford that or offer to pay for any damages that occur from one of your tenants. I wouldn't recommend doing any of these things unless you have to. By doing this, you're giving up unnecessary leverage to the owner. Who knows if they might have leased it to you like normal if you hadn't said anything. This is why it's better to let them reject you first before you offer to make any contingencies.

Where Should Your Sober Home be Located?

One of the most important aspects to a sober living home is going to be the location. Location by itself can make or break your business, depending on how you plan on operating things. For example, let's say you find a good deal on a home that's in a remote location. You decide to buy the property, but you don't offer transportation for anyone living in the home. You're now putting unnecessary constraints on the people who live in your home. It will be harder for them to find a job, and even if they do, how will they be able to reliably get there? You're setting them up for failure. On the same token, you could buy a home in a remote location and it winds up being a major success because you offer to provide transportation to your tenants. Also because it's in a remote location, there's less temptation, leading to an increased chance of people in the home staying clean. Again, this is why it's so important to think about the type of home that you want to have and how you want to run things. These decisions will act as the guiding light for your business. Let's say you don't want to offer your tenants transportation, then do you think that buying a home in a remote location is a good idea? No, in this case you need something that is in close proximity to essentials that the tenants will need. You'd need a location that is close to a bus stop or train station for transportation. Close to a grocery store and a gym for example. You want people to be put in a situation where it's easy for them to be successful. Think of it like saving for retirement. If you have things set up to where part of your income goes directly into your investment account, then things are easy. However, if you have to manually move the money yourself into the investment account, then there's a much better chance that it will get delayed and that it won't happen. Things are no different here when it comes to location and the success of your tenants. So, keep these things in mind when you're looking for a place for your sober living home.

What About Converting Your Personal Home into a Sober Living Home?

What if purchasing a home for this business is too much for you to handle right now? What if you're afraid to sign a lease or are struggling to find someone willing to take you up on it? Well, if you already own a home, you could use your personal space for this adventure. This won't be practical for everyone. You could have a family, in which case I would recommend avoiding this idea. You could own your home but live with a roommate, in which case they would have to be on board with this idea as well. Where is your home located? Is it in a good place for you to operate? You also have to consider the size of your home to a degree. If you live in a 3 bedroom home, your capacity would be 4 people, unless you wanted to share your own room, which I wouldn't recommend. However, if the situation is right, you could try this out if you really wanted to. You wouldn't have to pay anything extra for a lease or mortgage, which means that your profit margins would be significantly higher. You'd also be living with your tenants, which can make things easier to be more involved, if that's the type of house you want to run. You can test things out for as long or as little as you like without having to finish out a lease. You don't have to go through the stress of securing a loan or getting approval from someone else. There are some pros to it, so I wanted to throw the idea out there. The obvious downside is that people will be in your personal space 24 hours a day and there isn't any escaping it. If you're used to everything being yours, it can be a tough adjustment to have to start sharing. You also have to worry about your personal belongings. What are you comfortable with going missing and what are you not okay with losing. You need to properly secure your belongings to ensure they're not potentially stolen. If you're able to put the proper security measures in place, this isn't a bad idea to consider.

Business Entity and Business Insurance

Being that you are renting a property to a group of individuals, you need to have the right business establishment and insurance to give you peace of mind with your operation. As far as your entity of choice is concerned, more than likely starting an LLC is going to make the most sense. Anything could happen on your property. Someone could get injured due to the property not being maintained and you could be held liable. An LLC stands for limited liability company because it limits the liability that you would incur. It's very important to properly protect yourself when running this business and forming an LLC is the first way to do that. Now the question becomes, do you maintain one LLC or create multiple LLCs? You might think that you're forming one business and you technically are, but it can be smart to break things up. For instance, let's say you buy your first home and it's doing great. You're now ready to expand and open up your second home. This is where the decision starts. Do you list your second home under your current LLC or create a second LLC and list it under that LLC? You might think the answer is to list it under your original LLC. That can certainly provide some benefits. For one thing, it will be easier to track everything for tax and business purposes. However, I would advise against this in case you do face legal action. Make no mistake about it, LLCs will protect your personal belongings. However, your business assets are at stake. If you own two properties under the same LLC, both of your properties can be seized. If the properties are separated, then they can only go after the property where the incident occurred. Now, if you don't have a lot of equity in either property, then this seemingly isn't a big deal. You theoretically don't have much to lose. So it would seem simple enough to put both properties under the same LLC and continue to put additional properties under that same LLC. However, as time goes on, you will accumulate more equity and you will have more to lose. You can transfer your properties to their own LLCs, but you'll have a lot going on by that point. It's not something that has to get done, so you may delay and never get around to doing it. It's better to have things set up the right way from the jump to give you as much protection as possible. When it comes to stocks, common advice investors will give is to diversify your portfolio. This way if a certain market crashes, your portfolio isn't in complete shambles. It's the same line of thinking here with multiple LLCs. You're diversifying your assets so someone can't come after the whole pie if something were to happen. Now let's talk about insurance. There are a couple of different types of policies you're going to want to get to ensure a wide coverage against a long list of potential things that could go wrong. The first is going to be landlord's insurance, which as you can probably assume is for people who are renting out property for another person to live in. This type of insurance will help to protect both your property and protect you against liabilities that may occur on your property. The next kind of insurance policy you're going to want to look into is umbrella insurance. This is an additional liability policy that's meant to help cover you against things that your landlord's policy might not cover. This is why it's known as umbrella insurance. Much like an umbrella, it's meant to provide a wide variety of coverage for your business.

Americans with Disabilities Act

Something you need to be aware of with this business is the Americans with Disabilities Act. This law prevents people with disabilities from being discriminated against due to their status. Former drug users are considered protected under this act. This means you're not allowed to discriminate against housing someone because of their addiction and reasonable accommodations must be made. Reasonable accommodations would include things such as working utilities, having furniture, keeping appliances maintained, etc. Essentially what basics would you expect from living in your home? This law also comes into play in regards to evictions. However, one thing to note is the law protects against people with previous drug use. If drug use is current, then things change and the same protections aren't granted.

Zoning Regulations

A zoning regulation dictates how a specific piece of property in a certain area can be used. For instance, a city may not want two sober living homes within a certain amount of miles or feet within each other. For instance, that city may want a 5-mile radius between sober living homes. If a home already exists, then you would have to look to find a home outside of that radius. Zoning laws can be tricky because it varies depending on where you live. Due to the fact that people with a drug addiction past are protected under the Americans with Disabilities Act, zoning regulations may not be able to be applied. The bottom line is that zoning regulations may be a barrier for you and it might not be all depending on the location of where your home will be. One potential way you can get around this is by living outside of city limits. This can be of benefit to you if you were looking for a location that is more remote in the first place to help cut back on distractions.

Is a License Needed for a Sober Living Home?

This will come down to where you live once again. In some states, you'll only be allowed to provide housing. If you want to provide additional services, then you will need to be licensed. I recommend checking out the National Alliance for Recovery Residences (NARR) website at narronline.org to learn more information. They also have a certification program that you can learn more about as well.

Would You Live in Your Sober Living Home?

The last piece of advice I want to leave you with is to make the home inviting. Ask yourself if you would personally want to put your own family in this home. If your answer is no, then you need to put in some work into the place and make it look better. You might think that it doesn't matter. These people are struggling with addiction, and a roof over their head and a bed is better than nothing. That may be true, but providing a quality living space will give you many more benefits than saving a few dollars. For one thing, people will want to stay at your home. If they move out and relapse, guess where they're going to want to come back to?

That's right, they're going to come back to your home because of how nice it was. The chances of you receiving referrals will increase. People will talk about your home more because of the quality. Lastly, it gives your tenants a sense of pride. Oftentimes these people don't have much, so it's nice for them to be able to live in a place where they can stay clean and feel good about themselves. Now, this doesn't mean you have to go out and buy top-of-the-line furniture. In fact, you don't even have to buy new furniture. You should at least buy used furniture that looks like it is quality. If you wouldn't want to put a piece of furniture in your personal home, then don't put it in your recovery home. If the home looks outdated, see if there's a way for you to renovate the place. This will help to increase the value of the property so it can be a worthy investment. Part of having a quality home involves staying on top of repairs, so don't get lazy when it comes to that!

Chapter 4: House Rules How to Maintain Order in Your Home

Maintaining order in your home is going to be a big deal. This will directly relate to the amount of stress you'll have in this business. If things are out of control, then you'll regret your decision and look to get out as soon as possible. If you set up the right parameters, then things will be much smoother. It all comes down to setting your house up for success, and rules and structure are how you're going to do that.

Boundaries and Getting the Hands Occupied Are Key

Before I get into the details of some things you want to think about when establishing your house rules, I want you to understand the foundation of what leads to a successful home. Those two keys are boundaries and staying occupied. The better your home is at these two things, the easier your life will be. Boundaries are key not just for someone who's in recovery, but for everyone. Parents give their children curfews not because they want to control them but because it helps to keep them safe. They know that bad things happen the later in the night it gets. The same thing goes for your housemates. If parameters are set up to make theft more difficult, then the temptation won't be there. If housemates have their location tracked, then they know they'll be held accountable for wherever it is they're going. Boredom can become the other issue. There's an old phrase that says idle hands are the devil's workshop and there's a reason this quote exists. When people are bored, they look for a way to keep themselves occupied, and in the case of a recovery home, that could be regressing back into an old habit. If you can help to keep the people in your home engaged, then they'll be more likely to be successful in their recovery journey. This will help them when they move out of your home. They'll know how to keep themselves busy and will have less time for bad recreational activities. With these two ideas in place, let's now dive into the finer details about the type of parameters you should set up.

How to Prevent Theft in the Home

I'd love to be able to say that theft isn't something you'd have to worry about, but it sadly is. This isn't to say that everyone is going to be trying to steal when they get the chance. It's more so to be prepared for when someone would try to steal something. For certain things, you can not worry about it until it becomes an issue. Once it does, then you can start to take stricter measurements. Other things you're better off implementing right from the jump. The first example of this would be fridge locker boxes, assuming that each person has their own food and it isn't shared. This will allow everyone to keep their food separate. In this case, someone eating another housemate's food isn't that big of a deal, especially by comparison to other things that could happen. The food will be easy and cheap enough to replace if push comes to shove. This way you won't have to deal with any food locker boxes until it becomes an issue. If food theft becomes more of an occurrence than you want it to be, then go ahead and start implementing locker boxes to keep everyone's food separate.

The other thing you want to do to prevent theft is to give housemates a small lockbox that they can store valuables in such as ID cards, their wallet, or other items of value or importance to them. Each person will likely share a room with someone else, which leaves plenty of opportunity for something to get swiped. It will be fairly obvious if something large is taken or if a housemate is wearing someone else's clothes. If a ring is stolen, it can be a much different story.

Lastly, cameras will be a great way to not only hold people accountable for theft but also in general. You need to have doorbell cameras for the front and back doors. This way if someone tries to leave with an item that's a decent size, you'll be able to notice. You'll also be able to hold people accountable this way. You'll be able to know when someone left the home and when they came back to the home. Without this, it will be much harder to hold people accountable if you're trying to implement things like curfews.

Another security measure to put in place is a keyless door lock. You don't want to use a traditional lock and key because these keys can easily be replicated or lost. You also don't have to worry about retrieving a key from someone when they move out. You don't want to get a standard keyless entry pad though. You want to get one where you have remote access and can use multiple codes. The use of multiple codes allows you to assign a unique code to each person that lives in the home. You'll be able to know who came and left the home based on the code that was used. Then when someone moves out, you can just disable their code and you're good to go. Remote access means you can unlock and lock the door from anywhere as long as you have an internet connection. This can be good if you're trying to implement a curfew. You can make it known that the codes will be disabled after a certain time and their codes will not work. They'll have to contact you to be able to get back into the home after curfew has passed. These keypads will also let you see if the door is currently locked or unlocked, and it will provide timestamps every time the door is locked or unlocked. This way if another housemate unlocks the door from the inside, you'll be able to know since no code would be used to unlock the door. I recommend getting a keyless entry pad for both your front and back doors. If you implement a curfew, then what's to stop a housemate from unlocking the back door and letting them in? It will be easier for the housemates to get away with things if there isn't a proper security measure in place for any door entries. For your garage door, you can use a similar type of system where you'll have remote access and can see when the door was opened or closed. The other option you have is to not give access to your tenants to be able to open or close the garage door. This way it's one less thing that you have to worry about. As far as what brand you should consider, I recommend Eufy for a doorbell camera and smart lock. I like this brand because you don't have to pay a monthly fee for cloud storage. They're also reasonably priced compared to other brands on the market and it isn't low quality. For your garage, you can use something like myQ. However, there are plenty of other great options out there, so do your research and determine what you think will work best for you.

Use a Tracking App

The next way you can help to hold your housemates accountable is by using a tracking app, such as Life360. This app is really amazing because it will allow you to see the location of the person at all times. It will also give you notifications when their phone battery is getting low. This is just another measure you can take to help hold people accountable in their sobriety journey. You'll know if they're out late at night, and you'll know where they are. The other person will also know that they're being tracked, which will make it less likely that they'll try to do something they know they shouldn't.

Should You Provide Food?

Another consideration you're going to have to make for your recovery home is if you'll provide food for your home or if it will be up to the housemates to take care of that themselves. I would generally recommend against buying food for your home as this will greatly eat into your profits. It can also hinder growth because these people don't have to provide for themselves, they can just rely on you. On the other side though, some people may be struggling financially and really need the help. This is why it can be beneficial to partner with a local food bank to help supply your home with food. The other thing you can do is give people a card that a loved one can put money on for food. You can set things up in a way to where you have access to see the transactions and what the money is being spent on. If it's not being spent on food, then you can take the card away. If people don't like what's being offered from the food bank, then they can buy their own groceries or use their food stamp card if they happen to have one.

What Are Your House Rules?

You need to have house rules for people to follow so that they can be successful in their recovery journey. If you give complete and total control to people who are struggling with addiction, chances are that they will slip back into their old habits. Some of these rules may seem like you're treating these people like they are little kids. That is far from the case. Think about why a parent puts rules in place for their children, it's because they know what's best for them. If you tell a kid to brush their teeth, they won't do it. They'd eat a bunch of candy right before bed and not brush their teeth if it was up to them because they don't know any better. They don't know that the sugar will keep them up past their bedtime. They'll be tired the next day, and they won't be able to see how not brushing their teeth will cause cavities among other things. The parent however knows better. Sure the kid might not be happy about it, but the parent knows what's best for the child in the long run, which is why the rules are in place. The people living in your home aren't children, but the same premise will be helpful to them. When they have had complete freedom to do as they please in the past, it has led them to addiction. They need boundaries in place to prevent them from slipping back into their old ways. So here are some things you can consider implementing for your household:

Lights Out

You can implement a certain time of the day when the lights need to be turned off in the house and it's time for bed. That may seem like you're treating them like their kids, but remember, bad things happen late at night. By having a lights out policy, you can help to keep people out of trouble and help them establish a routine. The later people stay up, the worse off they're going to be the next day. Following a structured routine is a big key to staying clean, and having a lights out time is a great way to help with that.

No Weapons

You want to keep everyone in your home safe. In addition to that, you want other people in the home to feel safe. Anything could happen, and it's best to take the necessary preventive measures to ensure safety. Sure, people are normally allowed to keep certain weapons in their home for self-defense, but this is much different. Someone could very well go off the rails and use a weapon that's in the home to cause serious harm to a housemate. The weapon might not even be theirs. All of this can be prevented if you implement a no weapons in the house rule.

No Harassment or Discrimination

You also want your housemates to feel safe against harassment and discrimination. You need to make it known that these things are not acceptable and can result in eviction from the home. You want your home to be a positive environment so that people can work on improving themselves. It's hard to do that when someone is being a bully in the home. When someone is being harrassed, it can make them get down on themselves and potentially cause a relapse, so you need to stay on top of this. Make it known that people can reach out to you at any time if they have a concern or if they need to report something, such as bad behavior. You can also have your house leader or another employee who's closer to the housemates keep an eye out for this type of behavior as well. If an incident of something like harassment is reported, it's important to look into it. If you shrug it off and think the issue wasn't that big, then it makes it seem like you don't care. The person who reported the matter will think there's no point, and then something big might happen and you won't hear about it because you didn't take action previously. You don't want to assume what's being reported is true either. Someone could make a false report in an attempt to get a different roommate or to get someone kicked out of the home. The best thing you can do is get both sides of the story, but do so one at a time. If you talk to both people at the same time, you're likely to get the two people just talking over each other. During your interrogation, ask each party if there were any witnesses to the event. If there was, then you'll want to talk to them as well. This will help to provide you with a source that's not directly involved with the situation, which can make them less biased.

How Often Will You Drug Test?

Drug testing is going to be one of your best forms of accountability. If someone knows they're going to be consistently drug tested, it doesn't give them much of an opportunity to sneak off and get high. The question is how often do you want to drug test everyone in the home? You could do something such as once per week or even twice per week. You might even be able to do a drug test once every two weeks. Something such as once per month is simply too sparse. People will know that they'll have time before their next drug test, so they'll go ahead and binge. If you do something such as once per week, people will be less likcly to test the limits. You could also be random with your drug tests, but still have them average out to a certain number of tests per month. For example, you might aim to give each person 4 drug tests per month. You don't necessarily have to give the person a drug test the same day of the week at roughly the same time. There could be a week where they don't get drug tested, and then there could be another week where they get drug tested twice in the same week. This is a great way to keep people on their toes as long as the average number of tests they take is still a good cadence, and they won't have time to try and fake their way through the test with something like synthetic urine. You could also have people take a test once they gain access to a new privilege. For instance, let's say they now have access to their car and are allowed to go out. As soon as they get back, you could drug test them to ensure they didn't take advantage of their newfound freedom.

Room Checks

Having room checks every so often is a must. How will you know if people are following the rules? They could easily sneak a knife into their room and you would never know it. They could easily have drugs in their room and you'd be clueless. The only way to truly know what's going on is to check. If you do room checks on a regular cadence, then it will be fairly easy for someone to hide something they don't want you to see. If the room checks are random and can be done at a random time, then everyone is going to be held accountable. A good time to complete a room check for someone is going to be when they're not at home. This way they can't see it coming at all and try to conceal something at the very last second. You'll want to check the person's medications as well to make sure they're not being abused. This isn't something you want to quickly rush through either. People will get very creative with where they hide things. So make sure you take your time and thoroughly search the room because you never know what you might find.

Applying to a Certain Number of Jobs Per Day

Getting a job can be a big part of the recovery process, as it can help to establish a routine. You can have your tenants set goals where they apply to a certain number of jobs per day. They can do this by applying on job board websites and you can have access to their account. This way you'll be able to see the number of jobs that they've applied to and don't have to worry about them making up numbers.

Cars at the Home?

Will you allow tenants to park their cars at the home or are they not allowed to have a car at the home? There are benefits and drawbacks to each option. If you allow people to have their car at the home, they can provide their own transportation for things such as a job, which is great and it's a weight off of your shoulders. However, having a car at the home makes it easier to get out and about, which means it's easier for the tenants to put themselves in front of temptation. One solution to this is to offer different privileges to people based on how long they've been in the home for and how their recovery process is going. For instance, if after 90 days someone is staying clean and doing everything they're supposed to, they would then be allowed to have their car at the home. You would still be tracking their location and implementing a curfew, but that could be a privilege they gain when compared to someone who just moved in and doesn't need the added temptation of being able to leave at a moment's notice.

What are the Consequences?

If you have rules in place, but no consequences for breaking those rules, then what good are the rules? People will trample all over them because they know nothing is going to come from it. Action needs to be taken when someone breaks a rule, and this will help to send a message to other people living in the house, the rules are there for a reason. Your punishment should vary depending on what rule of the house is broken. There are certain things that require a more severe punishment than others. For example, let's say someone brings a weapon into the home such as a gun. This is grounds for immediate eviction because this tenant is putting the lives of everyone else in the home in danger. What about theft? This would more so be a case-by-case basis because it depends on what ended up being stolen. Was it a case of someone eating someone else's food? That could very well be innocent enough. If someone's jewelry, money, or medications are missing, then this is a completely different story. This would be grounds for an eviction. The person who was stolen from won't feel safe knowing that the person who stole their belongings is still living in the home. It also shows the victim that you care more about money than taking care of their best interests. You don't want to give off that type of vibe. So what about for lesser offenses, such as failing to do a household chore or not making it back in time for curfew? In these cases, you can ground them from something such as their phone or something else that they value. It may seem like you're treating them like they're teenagers, but it's effective. Finally, what do you do in the event that someone fails a drug test? Well, this is up to your discretion. On one extreme, you could evict them. However, you probably are in the business because you believe in second chances. So something along the lines of stripping certain privileges such as electronics and access to their car if they have one could be more appropriate for failing a drug test the first time. You have to decide at what point enough is enough and kick someone out.

Household Chores

You don't want to hire a maid to clean your home. If you do that, you are missing out on a great opportunity for your tenants. The point of having your tenants clean the house and do other chores is not so that you can keep a clean home for free or try and control them. It all centers around routine and teaching them how to live life in the outside world. Most people have a job and they have to do household chores on a regular basis to maintain the home. Chores aren't a bad thing as they provide cleanliness and control to the home. Therefore, you need to establish a chore system with your tenants to help them establish a certain routine. Here are some different ideas of chores you could have your tenants complete:

-Vacuuming
-Cleaning Baseboards
-Cleaning Kitchen Countertops
-Dusting the Blinds
-Mowing the Yard
-Raking the Leaves
-Watering the Plants
-Cleaning the showers
-Mopping

You could essentially split these tasks up evenly amongst the tenants and have them complete them on a regular basis, such as once per week. You could then rotate the chores between the tenants to help keep things fresh and prevent them from doing the same thing over and over. You also need to decide what you want to do about chores such as laundry and dishes. Typically, it's best that each person handles their own laundry to ensure that people's clothes don't get mixed up accidentally. When it comes to dishes, you could have each person take care of their own dishes right after they use them, or that could be another chore on the list that someone has to take care of. When everyone has to take care of their own dishes, there tends to be less of a mess because people will have to do their dishes as soon as they can. If not, then this leads to confusion as to who's dishes are who's. More of a mess tends to accumulate if it's an assigned chore because people will use more dishes knowing it's not their week to clean them so they don't care. It comes down to you holding people responsible to not just do their chores for the week, but do them correctly. You don't want to see a pile of leaves in the yard that wasn't put into a bag. You don't want to see a lump of dust at the end of the baseboard. You want people to take pride and ownership in what they're doing just like someone would who's living in their own space.

Having a House Leader

Having a house leader is going to be an important thing to establish, especially if you are less involved with the home. Even if you are very involved with the home, things will inevitably slip through the cracks if you're not living there. This is where a house leader can come into play. Your house leader will be someone who's lived in the home for a while. It's someone that you've built trust with over time and haven't had any issues with. They've done exactly what they're supposed to do and they've been good in their recovery process. Your house leader will be your second set of eyes, so to speak. They'll be able to keep tabs on the house without you being there. You'll know about internal conflicts, chores that aren't getting done, people that aren't being a team player, and you'll know about people trying to break the rules. You'll want to give your house leader a benefit for taking on this role. The last thing you want is for the person to resent you for feeling like they're having to do more work for nothing. A good incentive you can give them is a discount on their rent. You might give them half off, for example, because the insights they'll provide you with will be far more valuable.

Hiring a Housing Manager

As you scale and take on more homes, you can hire a house manager. Essentially this person will take on what your role will be in the beginning. They'll run and manage the different homes and make sure that everything is running smoothly. They'll handle any issues in the home. Help move people in or out of the home. Ensure that rules are being followed and that chores are being done. They can also help with marketing the homes to help fill up empty beds. Hiring this role will mean that you're taking on a salary. You may not be able to take on a full salary, but the good news is that you don't have to hire until you're ready. When you have multiple homes, you will be bringing in more money. You can also adjust things to make it easier for you to afford their salary if need be. For example, you can offer them a small percentage of the revenue that each home they manage generates in exchange for taking a lower base salary. This benefits you because you'll only pay them more money if you're making more money. It benefits the employee because it encourages them to fill up spots in the home so that more money is being made and thus they make more. In terms of who your manager should be, it's not a bad idea to consider someone who has been a house leader for you. They'll know the ins and outs of what you expect from them. You'll know if they'll do a good job or not based on how they've been as a house leader for you. They've also struggled with addiction in the past so they can relate to people living in your homes. They might not have management experience, but you can train them the way you want and help develop them into the type of employee you desire for the role. Of course, you don't have to do this, it's just one place you can look for your hire. You can also look to your personal network, post on social media, or even post on a job board. In this case, you likely won't find someone who has had an addiction in the past and that's okay. That shouldn't be a requirement for the job. What you will want to look for is someone you know that you'll work well with. So you might look to someone in your network that may lack relevant experience, but has a solid work ethic and is easy to get along with. If you're looking to make a hire outside of your network, then it will be best to look at hiring someone who has relevant experience if possible. The main thing is to be patient. The wrong hire can easily rub your tenants the wrong way. You want someone who is caring and understanding, but who also won't let things slide. Once you do hire a manager, it's still a good idea to have house leaders. Your manager can't be everywhere all the time, so your house leaders will still be able to keep an eye on things when the manager isn't around.

Other Ideas to Implement

Aside from what I've mentioned thus far, there are some other things you should consider doing if you want to keep your housemates engaged.

Volunteer Work, Community Service, and Exercise

Something you can do is set up volunteer opportunities that the house participates in as a group every so often. This could be something such as once or twice per month, but it's a good way to keep busy with things and give back to the community. It helps to create positive feelings to be able to give back in a way that money can't buy. It's important for your house members to feel this impact and regularly volunteering is a great way to achieve this. If you do implement this, you want to make it mandatory or make it to where everyone has to volunteer a certain number of hours per month if it's not done as a group. If it's voluntary, then people aren't going to do it and they aren't going to see the fruit that it can provide. The same premise follows with exercise. Exercising releases endorphins and it energizes us and makes us feel good. If there's a local gym, you could have housemates participate in a group exercise class. You might lead an at home workout every so often. The point of these activities is to help keep people engaged so that they're not bored and letting their mind slip back into addiction.

Game Nights and Weekly Meetings

I don't know about you, but I love game nights. They're so much fun and you can play a wide variety of games over time. Hours will go by without me even looking at the clock, and that's not just the case for me. This is why it's a good idea to have a weekly game night for similar reasons to the other things that I just mentioned. Weekly meetings are another thing that you should do. This will allow people the chance to air out any problems or concerns they have. It will also help give you some insights into the pulse of the home and be a good opportunity for the tenants to interact with each other. I recommend starting off the meeting with any points you need to bring up. Maybe there's a new rule you need to implement or a change that's going to be made. You might have to reiterate something that simply isn't being followed or go over any general announcements. Then you can open up the floor and ask the tenants if they have any questions, comments, or concerns that they would like to make. When doing this, things can get out of hand sometimes, but remember you're in charge, so keep control. Don't be afraid to interrupt people if things go off the rails. Also let it be known how long the meeting will be, such as an hour, for example. Then you can give updates as to how much time is left in the meeting. This way people will be more understanding when it's time to let someone else speak because everyone needs the opportunity to say something if they want to.

Give Them a Sense of Ownership

Earlier I talked about how it's important to not put more than 2 people in a room in most cases. You want these people to have their own space and take pride in it. You want to think of other ways you can achieve the same type of result. When people take pride in what they do, they'll be more involved because they're having a bigger role in whatever the activity is. This is why it's important to let the tenants plan game nights or to let them plan some other type of activity. Give them a plant that is theirs to take care of solely or something else along those lines. Doing these types of things will create ownership within your tenants and it will help them be more involved with the activities you're trying to get them to do. For instance, on game night, they'll choose the games that are to be played. It may sound trivial, but it goes a long way. People want to be in control and they want to be able to make decisions, and small things like this are a great way to achieve that.

Goal Setting and Target Move-Out Date

It's important for your housemates to set goals because it can help give them something they can work towards. For instance, you could have them set goals for when they'd like to move out, when they'll have a job, and even steps they'll take to stay out of harm's way so they can stay clean. The easiest way to do this is to have them attach a target date to the goal, and then have them write out the steps they'll take to be able to achieve that goal. For instance, they might set a goal to get a job within the first month of moving into the home. They'll do this by applying to 10 jobs per day 5 days a week until a job is obtained.

Transition People Who Have Lived in the Home for a Longer Period of Time

The last thing I want to talk about in this chapter is granting different privileges based on how long a person has lived in the home. For instance, you could create different phases that each last 90 days. If someone stays clean, does their chores, and is a willing participant in group activities, then they're able to move into the phase where they will be granted more privileges. For instance, you might not allow people to have their cars on the property when people first move in. As an example, if after 90 or 180 days everything has been going smoothly for someone, you would allow this person to have their car at the house and will do the same for other tenants once they reach that point. Their curfew time could be later or they might not have to take drug tests as often as people just moving in. This is of course completely optional for you to do. You can transition people who are making progress, or you can keep the rules the same for everyone at all times no matter what.

Chapter 5: When is the Right Time to Open a Second Home and Beyond While Maintaining Success in the First

If you can make a good chunk of money from one sober living home, why wouldn't you rinse and repeat so that you could make even more money? You obviously would as long as you could manage it without things falling apart. So how do you know when the right time is to consider opening a second home? You may never be interested in owning more than one transitional home and that's totally cool. If the idea does intrigue you, then you'll want to pay attention to this chapter.

Too Much Too Soon Leads to Old Habits

Would you recommend a tenant to go zero to 100 when they first move into your home? Would you have them applying to 100 jobs a day, completing household chores, planning group activities, etc. all within the first 24 hours of them moving in? No, that would be overwhelming. It would be too much to handle and it would make them doubt living there. They might move out soon afterwards or start to resent the home because they didn't have a chance to settle in. Things can turn out the same way with you. If you take on more than you can handle too soon, you'll start to resent what you do. It will become less about serving people and more about just trying to juggle everything that you have going on. If you're not able to keep up, then things will start to slip through the cracks and you won't even notice. Tenants will start to move out and you'll struggle to keep the beds full. You could end up in a situation where you end up worse off and it's all because you tried to grow before you were ready. So how do you know if you're ready to make the leap and open up your second home?

The Right Time to Open Up Your Second Home and Beyond

There's not going to be a specific day when everything is going to align perfectly and you'll just know it's time to open a second home. Instead, you'll have to use careful discernment to make this determination. It can be scary to take on a second asset because you have to start all over again with the process. Then once everything is finalized, you now have an empty home to fill. However, on the other side of that scary feeling is freedom. You can scale this up to the point where this is what you do full-time and make great money doing so. As long as you stay patient and move forward when you are ready, then you'll be good to go. So what indicators should you look to see if you're ready to open up your second home? Well, you need to take a close look and see how things are going with your first home. You want to be able to replicate the success your first home is having. You don't want to open a second home while you're still testing things out with your first home. Look and see what your turnover rate is. What's the average length of time that someone is staying in your home? If it's a short period of time such as 3 months, then that issue is only going to worsen with the second home because you'll be spread even thinner. Let's say you've struggled to even fill up the beds in your first home or that there's consistently internal conflict in the home and nobody follows the rules. All of these problems will present themselves in your next home because the bad habits will carry over. Don't assume it's just that you have bad tenants. If the right procedures aren't in place, then the same issues will eventually present themselves in every home that you open. The only problem is now these problems will be magnified. This is why you should wait until you have given yourself time to show that everything is running smoothly. If everything is being handled well for a decent period of time, then you can begin the process of getting your second home. When I say a decent time period, I'm talking about at least 6 months. You have to give the people some time to live in the home to truly know how good or bad things are going. You also want to think about how much cash you have on reserve. Even if you have a good track record of things going smoothly in the home, that's not the only factor you have to think about. How much cash do you have on reserve? If your beds went empty tomorrow and no one was paying you rent, how long would you be able to continue paying the mortgage? Ideally, you'd want to have at least 6-12 months of cash reserves on hand before you try and open your second home. Now that you'd have a second home, it's that much more maintenance and repairs you have to think about in addition to keeping your beds full. The cash reserves will help you get by in case one home has a bit of a lull. Finally, remember to open the second home under its own LLC to keep it as a separate asset from your first home.

What is the Ultimate Goal?

Aside from the advice above, the other thing I want you to think about is your long-term vision. I want you to remember back to why you wanted to start a sober living home in the first place. Is your main motivation the money or the impact? If it is the money, which is totally fine, just be aware of that. The money can sometimes cause us to make irrational decisions because we have tunnel vision for the money. Things start to get rushed and the quality of the housing will decline. So just be sure to take a rational look at the numbers before you make any big decisions.

Conclusion

Starting your own recovery home is one of the most rewarding things that you can do. I can tell you that there isn't a much better feeling than to see people blossom under something that you helped to create. On top of the impact, sober living homes allow you to make the most money from your home, so this business truly is a win-win. However, in order to get that win-win, you have to be willing to take the plunge. It will be challenging at times. You will be fearful at other times. I want you to know these things ahead of time so that you can continue pushing forward when times get tough. Just remember that tough times are temporary, but your impact on someone can last a lifetime!